Owl Be Busy All Week!

Cute Weekly Planner

Activinotes

Activinotes

DAILY JOURNALS, PLANNERS, NOTEBOOKS AND OTHER BLANK BOOKS

Copyright 2016

Weekly Planner

MONDAY	TUESDAY	WEDNESDAY
THURSDAY	FRIDAY	SATURDAY
SUNDAY		

Notes :

Weekly Planner

Weekly Planner

Weekly Planner

MONDAY	TUESDAY	WEDNESDAY
THURSDAY	FRIDAY	SATURDAY

SUNDAY

Notes :

Weekly Planner

Weekly Planner

Weekly Planner

MONDAY	TUESDAY	WEDNESDAY
THURSDAY	FRIDAY	SATURDAY

SUNDAY

Notes :

Weekly Planner

Weekly Planner

_____
_____
_____
_____
_____
_____
_____
_____
_____
_____
_____
_____
_____
_____
_____
_____
_____
_____

Weekly Planner

MONDAY	TUESDAY	WEDNESDAY
THURSDAY	FRIDAY	SATURDAY

SUNDAY

Notes:

Weekly Planner

Weekly Planner

Weekly Planner

MONDAY	TUESDAY	WEDNESDAY
THURSDAY	FRIDAY	SATURDAY

SUNDAY

Notes :

Weekly Planner

Weekly Planner

_____
_____
_____
_____
_____
_____
_____
_____
_____
_____
_____
_____
_____
_____
_____
_____
_____
_____
_____
_____

Weekly Planner

MONDAY	TUESDAY	WEDNESDAY
THURSDAY	FRIDAY	SATURDAY

SUNDAY

Notes:

Weekly Planner

Weekly Planner

 # Weekly Planner

MONDAY	TUESDAY	WEDNESDAY
THURSDAY	FRIDAY	SATURDAY

SUNDAY

Notes :

Weekly Planner

Weekly Planner

Weekly Planner

MONDAY	TUESDAY	WEDNESDAY
THURSDAY	FRIDAY	SATURDAY

SUNDAY

Notes :

Weekly Planner

Weekly Planner

 # Weekly Planner

MONDAY	TUESDAY	WEDNESDAY
THURSDAY	FRIDAY	SATURDAY

SUNDAY

Notes :

Weekly Planner

Weekly Planner

 # Weekly Planner

MONDAY	TUESDAY	WEDNESDAY
THURSDAY	FRIDAY	SATURDAY

SUNDAY

Notes :

Weekly Planner

Weekly Planner

 # Weekly Planner

MONDAY	TUESDAY	WEDNESDAY
THURSDAY	FRIDAY	SATURDAY

SUNDAY

Notes :

Weekly Planner

Weekly Planner

_____
_____
_____
_____
_____
_____
_____
_____
_____
_____
_____
_____
_____
_____
_____
_____
_____
_____

Weekly Planner

MONDAY	TUESDAY	WEDNESDAY
THURSDAY	FRIDAY	SATURDAY

SUNDAY

Notes:

Weekly Planner

Weekly Planner

 # Weekly Planner

MONDAY	TUESDAY	WEDNESDAY
THURSDAY	FRIDAY	SATURDAY

SUNDAY

Notes :

Weekly Planner

Weekly Planner

_____
_____
_____
_____
_____
_____
_____
_____
_____
_____
_____
_____
_____
_____
_____
_____
_____
_____
_____

Weekly Planner

MONDAY	TUESDAY	WEDNESDAY
THURSDAY	FRIDAY	SATURDAY

SUNDAY

Notes :

Weekly Planner

Weekly Planner

 # Weekly Planner

MONDAY	TUESDAY	WEDNESDAY
THURSDAY	FRIDAY	SATURDAY

SUNDAY

Notes :

Weekly Planner

Weekly Planner

 # Weekly Planner

MONDAY	TUESDAY	WEDNESDAY
THURSDAY	FRIDAY	SATURDAY

SUNDAY

Notes :

Weekly Planner

Weekly Planner

_____
_____
_____
_____
_____
_____
_____
_____
_____
_____
_____
_____
_____
_____
_____
_____
_____
_____

 # Weekly Planner

MONDAY	TUESDAY	WEDNESDAY
THURSDAY	FRIDAY	SATURDAY

SUNDAY

Notes :

Weekly Planner

Weekly Planner

Weekly Planner

MONDAY	TUESDAY	WEDNESDAY
THURSDAY	FRIDAY	SATURDAY

SUNDAY

Notes :

Weekly Planner

Weekly Planner

_____
_____
_____
_____
_____
_____
_____
_____
_____
_____
_____
_____
_____
_____
_____
_____
_____
_____

Weekly Planner

MONDAY	TUESDAY	WEDNESDAY
THURSDAY	FRIDAY	SATURDAY

SUNDAY

Notes:

Weekly Planner

Weekly Planner

Weekly Planner

MONDAY	TUESDAY	WEDNESDAY
THURSDAY	FRIDAY	SATURDAY

SUNDAY

Notes :

Weekly Planner

Weekly Planner

 # Weekly Planner

MONDAY	TUESDAY	WEDNESDAY
THURSDAY	FRIDAY	SATURDAY

SUNDAY

Notes:

Weekly Planner

Weekly Planner

Weekly Planner

MONDAY	TUESDAY	WEDNESDAY

THURSDAY	FRIDAY	SATURDAY

SUNDAY

Notes :

Weekly Planner

Weekly Planner

MONDAY	TUESDAY	WEDNESDAY
THURSDAY	FRIDAY	SATURDAY
SUNDAY		

Notes:

Weekly Planner

Weekly Planner

Weekly Planner

MONDAY	TUESDAY	WEDNESDAY
THURSDAY	FRIDAY	SATURDAY

SUNDAY

Notes :

Weekly Planner

Weekly Planner

Weekly Planner

MONDAY	TUESDAY	WEDNESDAY
THURSDAY	FRIDAY	SATURDAY

SUNDAY

Notes :

Weekly Planner

Weekly Planner

 # Weekly Planner

MONDAY	TUESDAY	WEDNESDAY
THURSDAY	FRIDAY	SATURDAY

SUNDAY

Notes :

Weekly Planner

Weekly Planner

_____

_____

_____

_____

_____

_____

_____

_____

_____

_____

_____

_____

_____

_____

_____

_____

 # Weekly Planner

MONDAY	TUESDAY	WEDNESDAY
THURSDAY	FRIDAY	SATURDAY

SUNDAY

Notes :

Weekly Planner

Weekly Planner

Weekly Planner

MONDAY	TUESDAY	WEDNESDAY
THURSDAY	FRIDAY	SATURDAY

SUNDAY

Notes:

Weekly Planner

Weekly Planner

Weekly Planner

MONDAY	TUESDAY	WEDNESDAY
THURSDAY	FRIDAY	SATURDAY

SUNDAY

Notes:

Weekly Planner

Weekly Planner

_____
_____
_____
_____
_____
_____
_____
_____
_____
_____
_____
_____
_____
_____
_____
_____
_____

Weekly Planner

MONDAY	TUESDAY	WEDNESDAY
THURSDAY	FRIDAY	SATURDAY

SUNDAY

Notes:

Weekly Planner

Weekly Planner

Weekly Planner

MONDAY	TUESDAY	WEDNESDAY
THURSDAY	FRIDAY	SATURDAY

SUNDAY

Notes :

Weekly Planner

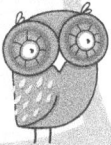

Weekly Planner

Weekly Planner

MONDAY	TUESDAY	WEDNESDAY
THURSDAY	FRIDAY	SATURDAY

SUNDAY

Notes:

Weekly Planner

Weekly Planner

 # Weekly Planner

MONDAY	TUESDAY	WEDNESDAY
THURSDAY	FRIDAY	SATURDAY

SUNDAY

Notes :

Weekly Planner

Weekly Planner

Weekly Planner

MONDAY	TUESDAY	WEDNESDAY
THURSDAY	FRIDAY	SATURDAY

SUNDAY

Notes:

Weekly Planner

Weekly Planner

Notes

www.ingramcontent.com/pod-product-compliance
Lightning Source LLC
Chambersburg PA
CBHW081335090426
42737CB00017B/3159